The Seven Bojjhaṅgās
The Buddhist Factors of Enlightenment
The Jhānas and
Days of the Week Buddha Images

The Seven Bojjhaṅgās
The Buddhist Factors of Enlightenment
The Jhānas and
Days of the Week Buddha Images

Paul Dennison

London, 2020

For more information, address:
www.pauldennisonpsychotherapy.co.uk

First hardback standard edition July 2020

ISBN 978-1-8380998-4-8 (hardback)

Itipiso Publications
pd@itipiso.org

Preface

In Thailand and some other Buddhist countries there is a tradition of associating a particular Buddha Image (Buddha Rūpa) to a day of the week, and many temples have a set of 7 images in front of which individuals, children and adults alike, may make an offering, *puja*, before the image corresponding to the day of the week on which they were born, particularly when they know the temple needs their support. That day is known to pretty well everyone born in Buddhist countries, in contrast to Western cultures where the date is more important.

There is also a tradition of linking each day of the week to one of the Bojjhaṅgās, the Factors of Enlightenment, or realisation, which characterise the Buddhist Path, but the details of how these two traditions developed and interact, and how each Buddha Rūpa relates to the Bojjhaṅgā for that day has become confused over the centuries with little written down.

The Bojjhaṅgās are very ancient, direct teachings of the Buddha over 2500 years ago, and recorded in Suttas composed during the approximately 200 years after his death up to the reign of the Indian Emperor Asoka. They comprise seven factors that together make up the Buddhist Path to understanding the nature of human suffering – its arising, causes, ending, and the Path to its end.

They are deeply embedded into Buddhist popular culture, chanted not only for recollection of the Path to Enlightenment, but also for healing, either for oneself or others. They are also closely related to the development of the jhānas, esoteric Buddhist meditation practices that allow a meditator to temporarily disengage from the limitations of the human everyday sensory consciousness to facilitate insight and direct understanding.

This book is a personal exploration of these interrelationships, informed in part by recent developments in understanding the neuroscience of jhāna. This *Neurodhamma* perspective will be new to most readers, and may take time to digest, but please be patient with it!

The book also describes some of the history of samatha and jhāna meditation; how large parts of the old traditions were suppressed and almost lost during modernisation reforms in Thailand and Burma, beginning in the early 1800s and then renewed with heavy promotion of "new vipassanā" in the 1950s. Understandings of jhāna meditation are only now being re-established in the West in new societal contexts, and with powerful cross-discipline and cross-millennial resonances between ancient Buddhist traditions and modern developments in neuroscience.

Online talks related to this monograph can be accessed here, https://www.samatha.org/bojjhangas-talks

Contents

1 Sati

Mindfulness, Monday

Wat Salaloi, Nakhon Ratchasima, Thailand (20th century)

In Buddhist popular culture, the story behind this image is an occasion where the Buddha was called to intervene to pacify arguing relatives. The posture is that of the Abhaya Mudra, where abhaya in both Sanskrit and Pāli denotes fearlessness and safety. It also represents mastery over passions, a moment where, confronted by anger or fear, mindfulness may be established with a return to reality and balance. Two versions of this image are seen in temples, one with a single hand raised and, slightly less common, this two-handed version, showing the double Abhaya Mudra.

From the perspective of Buddhist meditation and in relation to the Bojjhaṅgās, the mudra signifies that moment of mindfulness when Sati establishes a reference point in time and space free, at least temporarily, from sensory consciousness and the habits of greed, hatred and delusion. As will be described later, it may start very simply by a conscious act of re-directing attention to the breath in meditation, resisting the habitual pulls of sensory consciousness and entanglement in thinking, liking and disliking.

For a person born on any particular day of the week, it is considered in this tradition that the corresponding Bojjhaṅgā might carry some special significance. The Monday-born person might be naturally mindful, for example; on the other hand they might not, maybe even careless and unmindful, in which case Sati would be something to develop.

Factors or Stages

Sati traditionally appears first in a list of the Bojjhaṅgās, but this does not necessarily imply that the Bojjhaṅgās are to be developed in a rigid sequence. At times a person might be drawn to consider or try to develop one in particular, before moving forwards again, or temporarily backwards, through the seven factors until eventually a sense of the whole begins to appear.

It's as though the Bojjhaṅgās, and to a similar degree the

rūpa and arūpa jhānas which will be described later, form a kind of matrix which can be internalised as a picture of the Buddhist Path. On the fine-material level of jhāna meditation – by which is meant the felt, metaphorical and symbolic level, as opposed to the merely cognitive verbal level – we might say these factors act as a kind of visualisation of the whole endeavour a person undertakes when they begin meditation.

In practice, development of any of the Bojjhaṅgās must start very simply; if a person were to aim too high they risk trying to develop an intellectual construct rather than a quality rooted in direct experience. This is especially important for the first Bojjhaṅgā, Sati, which in meditation establishes a starting point, a marker, for all that follows, the rest of the meditative journey. This is not unlike beginning a journey by car by entering a postcode in the Satnav so that the software can work out how to get from A to B. If we don't know where we are to begin with, we risk going in circles, or becoming lost.

Sati, as a starting point, is an act of mindfulness, or recollection, of where we are. It establishes a point of self-awareness in a very basic sense – a kind of waking-up – with a location in time and space. The placing of attention is a moment in time, and as embodied beings our awareness is automatically "oriented" in space. Beginning meditation, this equates to a simple and clearly defined mental act of placing attention on the object of meditation. In *ānāpānasati*, mindfulness of in- and out-breathing which will be taken as our model of meditation throughout this monograph, the first stage of practice takes the form of mentally counting during in- and out-breaths, where each number in turn becomes the object of attention, of Sati (for more on ānāpānasati see Thich Nhat Hanh, 2008) .

From such simple beginnings, Sati progressively deepens over time as the other Bojjhaṅgās come into play interactively, eventually reaching completion as all-encompassing Sati, the 7th

factor of the Buddhist Eightfold Path, *Sammā Sati* (see final chapter). This is an important point, that the Bojjhaṅgās are factors that develop progressively, and interactively, rather than being fixed qualities.

The Human Default Sensory Consciousness

The Bojjhaṅgās together describe the entirety of the Buddhist Path of development, and an integral part of that Path is development of the jhānas, four on the level of "form", the rūpa jhānas, and four formless or arūpa jhānas (Brahmāli, 2007). In this book we only consider the rūpa jhānas as they relate to the Bojjhaṅgās.

In Buddhist Suttas the attainment and experience of the 1st rūpa jhāna is described, in Pāli, as:

vivicc' eva kāmehi paṭhamaṃ jhānaṃ upasaṃpajja vihārati
"Apart from sense desires, attains and dwells in the 1st jhāna"

When we come to look at the neuroscience of jhāna, we will see that the phrase "vivicc' eva kāmehi" describes disengagement from our habitual default sensory consciousness, a realisation that has only become clear through recent studies of the brain activity of meditators developing jhāna (Dennison, 2019). The meditator redirects attention inwards, eventually towards the mind itself. The resulting jhānas, sometimes described as states of absorption, are stages of increasing simplicity and stillness where, without the distractions of sensory consciousness, insight into the nature of reality may be achieved.

The word "vihārati" in the quote above is often used to denote the dwelling place of a monk or nun in a Buddhist temple, while in this case it denotes a new dwelling in jhāna consciousness rather than sensory consciousness.

The everyday consciousness we all live within from birth, is reflected in a dynamic balance of activity within the brain, between sensory inputs from the outer world as well as inputs from the body itself, all processed at a mostly unconscious level in relation to previous experiences held in memory, to predict possible outcomes leading to choices of action. This consciousness was named in Dennison (2019) as the human default sensory consciousness, and corresponds to those brain networks described in modern neuroscience that interact through processes of adaptive active inference to support our ongoing sense of identity (Seth and Friston, 2016).

The relevance of all this to Sati, is that from the point of establishing mindfulness in meditation and turning attention inwards away from the cognitive processes of our default consciousness, characterised by "naming", differentiating "this" from "that", including processes of liking or disliking, then it is possible to see changes in brain activity that represent disruptions of sensory consciousness networks.

Sati and Attention

Taking ānāpānasati meditation as the example, different lengths of breath are used in the first stage of "counting". In the tradition that informs this book (https://www.samatha.org), the longest length is counted as 1 to 9 on the in-breath and back down 9 to 1 on the out-breath. Moments when a meditator mentally sounds "1", "2", "3" etc., establish markers in time within the space of the in- and out-breaths. The moments of contact with each number are moments of active focused attention, representing concentration, while the maintenance and awareness of the length of breath keeps mindfulness going.

At first this is a cognitive process, not yet separated from sensory consciousness. It has a time-course to support our ongoing sense of being conscious of "something", and it unfolds and repeats so long as we remain entangled within sensory consciousness. In neuroscience this process is represented by the dorsal and ventral attention/perception streams in the brain's network activity (Petersen and Posner, 2012; Milner, 2017).

The dorsal stream (Figure 1) links the visual cortex at the back of the head, via parietal cortex areas across the top of the head (hence dorsal, as in the dorsal fin of a shark), to frontal areas of the brain. In Dennison (2019), the posterior and frontal sites were hypothesised to represent the subject ("I"/Eye; visual cortex) and object (cognitive detail; frontal cortex) poles of sensory consciousness.

The dorsal stream carries mostly moment-to-moment information, is therefore short-term and not, or very minimally, connected to long-term memory. It establishes location in time and space, and in neuroscience is often referred to as the "where" pathway. It is also egocentric as opposed to allocentric (salience and meaning), which will become relevant when we come to discuss the second Bojjhaṅgā, Dhamma-vicaya.

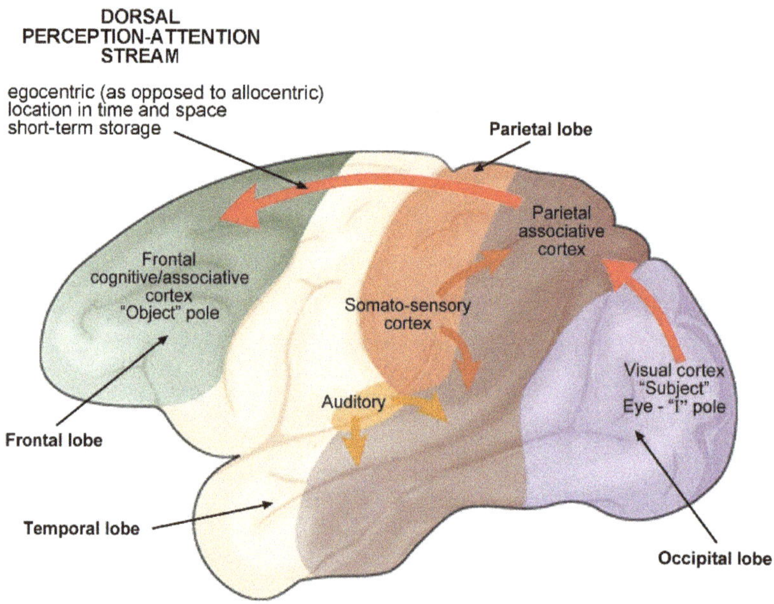

Figure 1 The dorsal attention/perception stream in the human brain

In terms of meditation and development of the first jhāna, the dorsal stream corresponds to the first jhāna factor, vitakka, often translated from the Pāli as "placing attention".

The counting stage in ānāpānasati meditation is a simple mental act of placing attention, the starting point for developing Sati. The second stage of ānāpānasati is termed "following", where the meditator attempts to feel the sensations of the breath, as continuously as possible, as it moves in from the nose tip, down through the throat into the chest and diaphragm; and then the reverse sensations on the out-breath.

This requires a much greater awareness of sensation and feelings, adding a quality of salience to mindfulness, which leads to the second Bojjhaṅgā, Dhamma-vicaya, or investigation (of dhammas and meaning).

2 Dhamma-vicaya
Investigation of Dhammas
Tuesday

Buddha in Parinibbāna, 8th/9th century
Wat Khooha, Kanchanadit, Surat Thani, Thailand

The second Bojjhaṅgā, Dhamma-vicaya, is generally translated as "investigation of dhammas", where dhammas can be understood as "reality", or anything that pertains to our ongoing body-mind experiences as human beings. In some Buddhist Suttas, dhamma-vicaya is described as "discriminating Dhamma with wisdom".

This factor is associated with Tuesday, and the Buddha Rūpa (image, form) for Tuesday is the reclining Buddha. Some of the most beautiful Buddha images are found in caves, and the example shown is a magnificent and immense reclining Buddha found in the cave temple, Wat Khooha, in Surat Thani province, Thailand, dating from the $8^{th}/9^{th}$ century Srivichaya period.

There are two views as to the significance of this posture in the day-of-the-week tradition. One, in popular culture, relates to an occasion when the Buddha was approached by a giant *Asura*, (a lesser god, or Titan) full of pride, and how the Buddha adopted the reclining posture and made himself larger than the Asura as a sign to the Asura to let go of his pride.

A second view, more appropriate to the Bojjhaṅgā tradition, relates the image to the last days of the Buddha when he adopted this posture in his Parinibbāna. Towards the end, the Buddha asked his followers, three times, if they had any last questions or doubts regarding his teachings. Each time his followers remained silent, confirming that the Buddha had taught the Buddha Dhamma to completion, that, in effect, Dhamma-vicaya (all questions; all investigation) was now complete, not only for the Buddha but for his followers too.

Significance for Persons Born on a Tuesday

The obvious question for a Tuesday-born person would be whether they might have a special affinity to some quality of investigation or discrimination; or on the contrary, might they benefit from more effort in that direction?

In exploring this with groups of meditators, one of the themes that often emerges is that of two broad character types among those drawn to meditation. One group are drawn to investigation *before* practicing, and find group dhamma discussions, listening to dhamma talks, or reading texts on meditation very helpful in giving some form of orientation and direction, and a degree of confidence, before wholeheartedly taking up meditation. The other category finds too much of such activities a hindrance, and much prefer to "dive in" and learn by doing. After such direct experience, however, persons in this category can also find dhamma investigation deeply satisfying.

Some Buddhist teachers have described these character types as "vipassanā leads samatha" (or insight leads tranquillity), and "samatha leads vipassanā" (or tranquillity leads insight), respectively. For more on samatha meditation see Wallace (1999).

A lesson to learn from this is that no matter what day of the week one is born, whether there are special affinities or not, there is something fascinating in exploring the different qualities and personal resonances that the day of the week tradition evokes.

The Inter-Relatedness of the Bojjhaṅgās

Sometimes the "investigation" of dhamma-vicaya is understood as discriminating between wholesome and unwholesome states, blameful and blameless states, inferior and superior, or good and evil states. This is a starting point, often as a form of dhamma discussion outside meditation, and in that sense similar to the basic starting point of placing attention when developing mindfulness, Sati. However, in meditation, dhamma-vicaya is less a cognitive process of investigation than a way of looking based on curiosity and a wish to understand. It goes beyond superficial or learnt meanings, or cultural assumptions based on personal experiences, and is ultimately more concerned with seeking "Truth".

Nai Boonman, the first teacher in the Samatha Trust tradition (https://www.samatha.org), once asked a group of University students in Cambridge, in 1965, whether they thought it possible to know right from wrong. His question led to much discussion and "views", which didn't appear to get anywhere, yet it planted a seed in some of his students regarding the difference between cognitively-based "ideas", as opposed to the possibility of direct intuition of Truth, essentially the heart of the Buddhist Path.

In that sense, just as Sati develops from simple first steps to become all-encompassing mindfulness, *Samma Sati*, so does Dhamma-vicaya develop progressively from curiosity and a search for meaning, into its fruition in truth and wisdom, *Pañña.*

The Neuroscience of Attention

The technique adopted in ānāpānasati meditation begins with mentally counting while breathing in and out, and the second stage is to follow and feel the sensations of the breath as continuously as possible during the in and out breaths. In the theory of jhāna meditation, counting develops the first jhāna factor vitakka, or "placing attention", and following the breath develops the second jhāna factor vicāra, or "sustained attention".

Most remarkably, this practice based on the introspective process of meditation dating back to the time of the Buddha, 2500 years ago and perhaps earlier, has a direct counterpart in modern neuroscience understandings of attention (see also: https://www.frontiersin.org/articles/10.3389/fnhum.2019.00178/full)

The dorsal attention stream of neuroscience was mentioned earlier in relation to Sati, and Figure 2 shows the full picture of *both* the dorsal and the ventral attention streams. The dorsal stream is fast and short-term, rather like the RAM in a computer, and establishes a position in time and space and corresponds well to the basic moment-to-moment function of placing attention in Sati, and the jhāna factor vittaka.

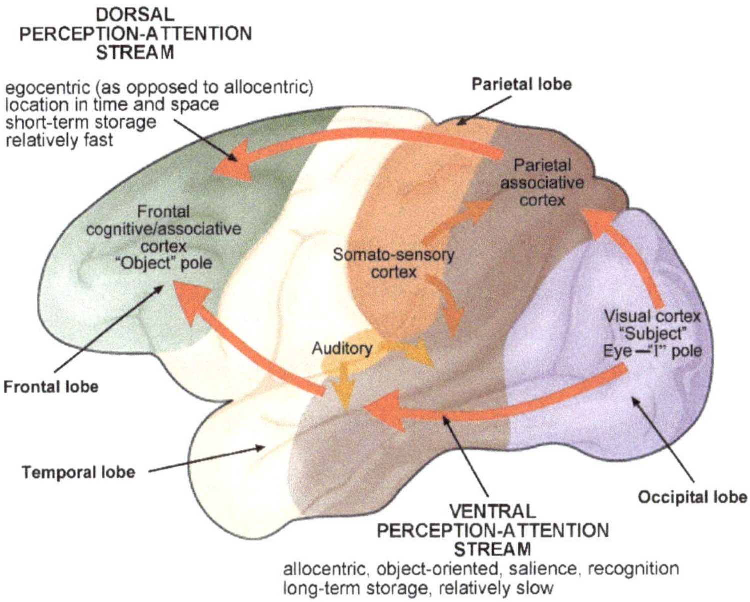

Figure 2 The dorsal and ventral attention/perception streams of neuroscience

The ventral stream also links posterior to frontal areas in the brain, but its route passes through core areas and the temporal lobe which have a range of functions including long-term memory, feelings and emotions, which together establish meaning and salience. In establishing meaning and salience, it links information in time and space, and therefore has a longer time scale. While the dorsal stream is sometimes referred to as the "where" stream, the ventral stream is referred to as the "what" stream, and corresponds well to the functions of Dhamma-vicaya and the jhāna factor vicāra.

These two attention/perception streams (Milner, 2017), and the cortical networks that support their activity, are the backbone of everyday sensory consciousness, and since the function of jhāna meditation is to temporarily disengage from sensory consciousness, we might expect disruptions to these two attentional processes in the brain as a meditator moves to develop Sati and Dhamma-vicaya, and in turn vitakka and vicāra and the 1st rūpa jhāna, which is indeed what is observed.

Recordings of Brain Activity when Developing Sati and Dhamma-vicaya and the 1st Rūpa Jhāna

From 2014-19, 30 practitioners of ānāpānasati meditation with a special interest in developing the jhānas, volunteered to have their electrical (EEG; electroencephalogram) brain activity recorded while meditating. This involved wearing head-caps with either 21 or 31 electrodes, the former wireless, connected to medical-grade amplifiers and analysis software.

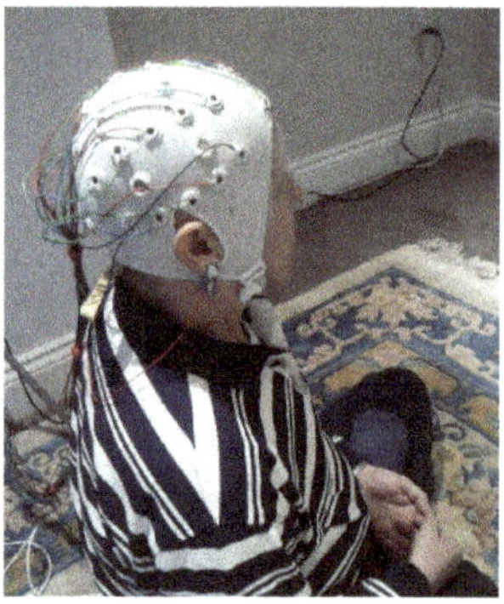

In normal life, if a person closes their eyes their EEG will show rhythmic but random "alpha" rhythms near the back of the head as a sign of a relaxed resting state. This alpha rhythm has an underlying time-scale of ~100 msec, or frequency ~10 Hz. The 100 msec corresponds to the minimum reaction time built into our biological systems. In many ways, the alpha rhythm is the "signature" of our everyday sensory consciousness; it represents the shortest time between a sensory stimulus and action, in effect, the minimum time to process a very basic "thought".

The top panel in Figure 3 shows a section from a 21-channel EEG recording of a meditator working to develop the 1st rūpa jhāna. The upper traces come from the front of the head, moving progressively down to the bottom traces from the back of the head. Strongly rhythmic alpha bursts can be seen at posterior electrode sites, and the expanded trace (middle panel) shows the characteristic and highly symmetrical wave-packet form of the alpha "spindles". The bottom panel for comparison shows the more random non-meditating resting-state alpha rhythm.

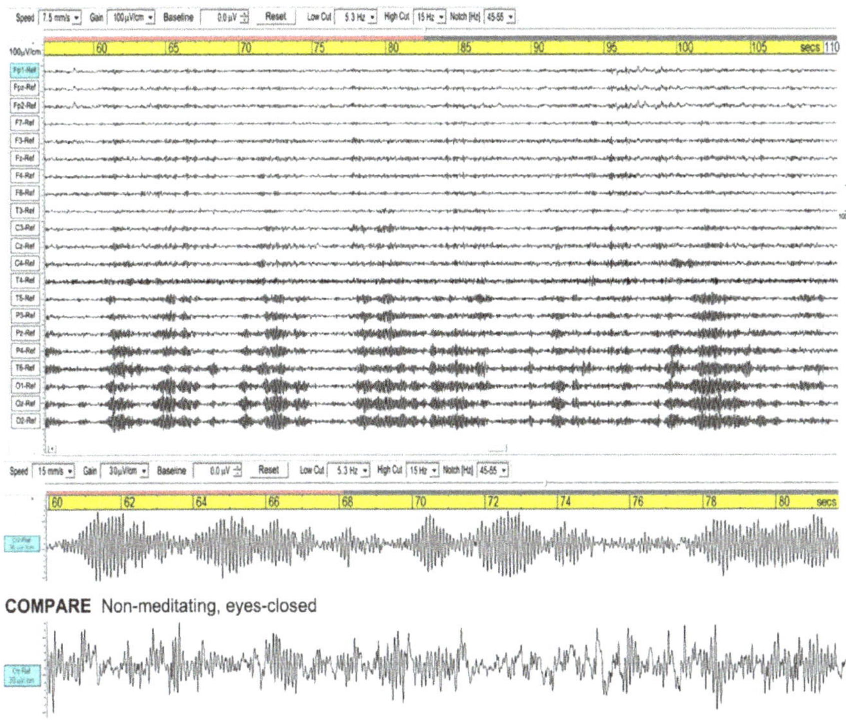

Figure 3 Top panel, a 21-channel EEG recording during meditation; middle panel, expanded signal at posterior site O2; bottom panel, a comparison to the non-meditating eyes-closed condition.

These alpha "spindles" correspond to disruption of the two dorsal and ventral attention/perception streams when meditators deliberately re-direct their attention inwards to disengage from their habitual sensory consciousness. Now it happens that spindles are well-known in neuroscience in the approach to deep sleep or anaesthesia, states verging on loss of consciousness, and these observations are unique in showing that the default attention networks in the brain can be disrupted while fully conscious by acts of redirecting attention during meditation. In the published EEG study, spindles were interpreted as the first signs of success for meditators developing vitakka and vicāra (and therefore the first two Bojjhaṅgās, Sati and Dhamma-vicaya) in approaching the 1st rūpa jhāna.

Completing the 1st Rūpa Jhāna

In the early years of establishing a samatha and jhāna tradition in England, 1965 or 1966, Nai Boonman was once asked by one of the monks assigned to the newly established Thai temple in London, "What do you teach?" This was a loaded question since Boonman was known to be a former monk from the traditional jhāna traditions that had been suppressed in Thailand during the 1950s by Burmese vipassanā. Whereas the new Thai temple and its monks were the now "modern face" of Buddhism, with its heavy promotion of vipassanā and implicit devaluation of samatha and jhāna practices. If Boonman were seen to be teaching any of the old practices, his position at the Thai Embassy where he was partly responsible for managing the new temple would likely have been compromised. So mostly he avoided questions such as this, preferring to keep a low profile.

On this occasion, to everyone's surprise, Boonman did answer, very simply, "I teach the first jhāna", without elaborating further; it may have been that this time he judged the monk to have a more genuine curiosity. Nevertheless, his answer is significant, since within the oral traditions surrounding the jhānas the 1st rūpa jhāna is considered the basis for all that follows, such that if someone experiences it, but for whatever reason does not practice further, it is believed they will invariably return to practice sometime later in life, or maybe in the next life.

The Buddha is perhaps the main example; when he exhausted all avenues of exploration after following the leading teachers of his time, he recalled as a young boy experiencing the deep peace of the 1st rūpa jhāna while watching his father take part in a ploughing ceremony, and determined from then on to relinquish austerities to follow the direction of developing the jhānas fully.

From a *Neurodhamma* perspective – to coin a new term – completion of the 1st rūpa jhāna marks temporary disengagement from sensory consciousness which, as we shall see, heralds unfoldment of the next three Bojjhaṅgās, as well as the higher jhānas. It is also regarded as a temporary experience of the first *Sotāpanna* stage of realization (Chapter 7).

3 Viriya
Vigour, Wednesday

Wat Chonglom, Ratchaburi, Thailand
~15th/16th century

The image for the third Bojjhaṅgā, Viriya, and for Wednesday, is the Buddha with bowl, "Phra Um Bhat". The associated story is that four years after his enlightenment the Buddha visited his birth family in Kapilavatthu, where his father was by then a regional King, but to the surprise of his relatives did not attend a banquet in his honour, and instead followed his practice of walking on an alms round. The image is of generosity, *dāna*, offering oneself as a field of merit for anyone, in turn, to offer food as the gift of extending life. It is also an image of *renunciation* – of attachment and of enmeshment in sensory consciousness. It implies a new direction away from sensory consciousness, a choice, and determination to see something through, a characteristic of Viriya as *vigour*; more than simply strength or energy.

Wat Bot Ratcha Decha, Ayuttaya, Thailand

The image of the Buddha with bowl is specifically linked to morning-born persons, and a second image is often used for those born in the evening depicting the Buddha receiving offerings from an elephant and a monkey. The same theme of receiving alms applies, but in this case, the image indicates generosity and compassion towards all beings, humans and animals alike.

Are persons born on a Wednesday naturally vigorous and energetic? Based on a quick survey of friends (that you may want to test out yourselves), it appears that some Wednesday persons, interestingly, tend to see themselves as sometimes, even often, quite lazy, while others might judge them to be rather driven.

A Monk's Alms Round, *Bindabat*

In a rural temple where the author stayed for most of 1992, there was an old monk who was renowned for never having missed an alms round, Bindabat, for more than 40 years, even though by that time he had bad rheumatism and arthritis. Since the Abbot was confined to a wheelchair, this monk had been the lead monk on the alms round for quite some years. One early morning, walking slowly and barefoot through a nearby town, the line of monks came to a stop. A man and wife, holding their young son, had already had their offerings of food accepted, and were now asking something of the old monk at the head of the line, who did not at first understand what was being asked of him. Apparently the little boy was sickly and not thriving, and no treatments so far had been able to help, and they were requesting a blessing by the old monk.

Finally he understood, and agreed, and with some assistance to support him, to make sure he didn't fall over, he placed his foot on the little boy's head, as requested, and chanted a blessing, as though it was the most natural thing in the world. Now many readers of this book will know, from visiting Southeast Asia, that it is a serious taboo to point your feet towards someone, certainly not towards the head, and absolutely not to touch the head with the feet. Yet in the eyes of the villagers this old monk's feet had become imbued with great magical power as a result of his unwavering Viriya over more than 40 years, completely transcending the mundane taboo.

Towards the 2nd Rūpa Jhāna

While the Sutta formula for the 1st rūpa jhāna highlights separation from sensory consciousness (vivicc' eva kāmehi), that for the 2nd rūpa jhāna,

vitakka-vicārānaṃ vūpasamā dutiyaṃ jhānaṃ upasaṃpajja vihārati
"With the calming of applied and sustained thought attains and dwells in the 2nd jhāna"

highlights the calming of applied and sustained thought, vitakka and vicāra (vitakka-vicārānaṃ vūpasamā), which are the key features of the 1st rūpa jhāna and which meditators strive to master in its development. As described in the last chapter, this equates to mastering the processes of attention.

However, the 1st rūpa jhāna is still close to sensory consciousness, and it is not uncommon that some meditators touch jhāna momentarily and hardly know it except for some degree of stillness and peace that may last for varying durations after emerging from their practice. Also, even if the 1st jhāna is experienced more fully, an inexperienced meditator may very likely become excited and immediately bounce out into sensory consciousness to think about the experience, and find it difficult to re-enter the jhāna. Usually meditators develop their understanding and practice in a natural way, but if not a nudge in the right direction by an experienced teacher may be needed. Paradoxically, the "right direction" is usually marked by a growing sense of being content with just where you are.

In fact, this is a key transition point, where meditators realise that the present moment is more satisfying than trying to do anything specific, or to "get anywhere". It is a more instinctive and "felt" state, rather than being cognitively-driven, and previous assumptions or attempts to think oneself into jhāna fade away. It is marked by Viriya – a growing confidence and conviction that a process might be seen through to eventual completion. It is also interesting that Viriya is much easier to recognise in others, rather than in oneself, as a patient yet determined commitment to see things through.

Invocation

The transition from sensory consciousness to jhāna consciousness takes time to get used to, with the gradual realisation that habitual cognitive processes of trying to think about jhāna, to conceptualise it, or to think oneself into it, are now hindrances to attaining the actual experience of jhāna consciousness. In practice this means that a meditator has to get used to what in jhāna terminology is referred to as the "fine-material" realm, where meaning is found in symbolic or metaphorical forms rather than conventional language.

In the oral Yogāvacara tradition (Bizot, 1992; Rhys Davids, 1896), formerly widespread for centuries across Southeast Asia, Invocation is used rather than any attempt to verbally construct what one wishes to experience. All practices begin by invoking the lineage of Buddha, Dhamma and Saṅgha, the lineage of teachers that followed, right up to a meditator's own teacher, to oneself, and in turn anyone you might yourself teach if you happen to be a teacher. The invocation, in essence, aims to invoke the entire Path to eventual realisation.

This is also related to Viriya; the sensing or invoking of a new direction or eventual Path, together with conviction to follow it through. In terms of the neuroscience of jhāna meditation, this stage is related to the growing confidence a meditator now has in resisting any pull back into the thinking, labelling and recognition habits of sensory consciousness. A meditator *holds* this position by direct experience, not conventional thought, until it eventually becomes automatic to not react to the merest hint of a pull back into thinking or recognition.

However, because the processes are now no longer crudely cognitive, and are not processed by language, the subtleties of how this is done are easily forgotten. This is balanced by a very important stage in meditation practice, *recollection*, where a meditator remains in stillness for a short while at the end of a meditation session, before re-engaging with the world, so that the quality and felt state – the fine-material state – is more easily available through recollection when he/she next comes to practice. This will be discussed in more detail in Chapter 6.

A Major Transition

The developing contentment mentioned above is the beginning of a process that leads to ever-deeper absorption, and eventually to the deep happiness or even bliss, *sukha*, characteristic of the 3rd rūpa jhāna. It also signals the processes of attention – vitakka and vicāra – becoming automatic, rather like how we learn to keep our balance when learning as children to ride a bike. At this point the 1st rūpa jhāna comes to completion, and vitakka and vicāra are no longer an active focus to be developed. However, rather than completely disappearing, they become part of the foundations that will support the development and new dwelling, vihāra, of the 2nd rūpa jhāna, and the meditator no longer needs to worry about them, in the same way we usually don't worry about the foundations of conventional houses we live in.

It was commented in the previous chapter that the 1st rūpa jhāna is regarded as crucial for any further progress in developing the higher jhānas, and since its development is intimately tied to the jhāna factors vitakka and vicāra, and the corresponding Bojjhaṅgās Sati and Dhamma-vicaya, it may be significant that the well-known Pāli chant for recollection of the Bojjhaṅgās, used widely in Southeast Asia, lists these first two factors together in the first line,

Bojjhaṅgo sati-saṅkhāto dhammānaṃ vicayo tathā
"The factors of awakening include mindfulness,
investigation of qualities"

The next three factors Viriya, Pīti and Passaddhi, which are closely interrelated in developing the 2nd rūpa jhāna, then appear together in the second line,

Viriyam pīti passaddhi bojjhaṅgā ca tathāpare
"vigour, exhilaration and tranquilisation"

while the 6th and 7th Bojjhaṅgās, Samādhi and Upekkhā, which are the key factors as will be seen later for the 3rd and 4th rūpa jhānas, respectively, appear in the third line,

Samādh'upekkha-bojjhaṅgā satt' ete sabba-dassinā
"and concentration and equanimity complete these factors."

Subjectively, it does indeed appear that establishment of the 1st rūpa jhāna is a major transition, and one that allows the following three Bojjhaṅgās to unfold interactively.

Looking ahead to the following chapters, Viriya becomes the driving force for what follows; and while "vigour" is probably the closest approximation to its meaning, it also has a quality of direction and in that sense is a *vector*, to borrow from scientific terminology.

The 4th Bojjhaṅgā, Pīti, also becomes active at this point, reflecting a much increased level of available energy; while the 5th Bojjhaṅgā, Passaddhi, corresponds to a necessary incorporation or tranquilisation of that energy into a mind-body samādhi that becomes the basis for the 3rd and 4th jhānas.

4 Piti

Exhilaration, Joy, Thursday

Bodh Gaya, India

The image for the 4th Bojjhaṅgā, Pīti, and for Thursday, is the Buddha under the Bodhi tree on the night of his enlightenment. According to tradition, the Buddha had resolved to sit under the Bodhi tree until completion of his task, no matter how long it might take; which is a statement of Viriya. It is then described that he overcame "Mara" (which, whether real or not, stands for the last vestiges of attachment to the sensory world). As a result he became suffused not only by Viriya, but also by Pīti and sukha (mental bliss), leading him to finally master all disturbances of body and mind through the jhānas to eventual Nibbāna.

In the core Buddhist traditions of both the Theravāda and Mahāyāna, Pīti has always been regarded as indispensible, and that without a significant development of Pīti it is simply not possible to master the 2nd and higher jhānas. In the oral Yogāvacara tradition, for example, as well as invoking the lineage of the Buddha, Dhamma, Saṅgha and teachers, as mentioned in the last chapter, the invocation also includes a wish that meditators experience *the full range of Pīti*, from minor signs such as the hairs of the body or head prickling, up to full flooding rapture causing the body to shake, swell and lift from the ground.

What is Pīti?

The descriptions in the invocation are very enigmatic, but what exactly is meant by the Pāli word Pīti? The most common translation historically has been "joy", yet in the Buddhist Abhidhamma (lit. higher dhamma or meta-dhamma) Pīti is not classified as a feeling, but rather as part of the formations, and is related to grasping the object (of meditation) with energised interest.

The EEG study of brain activity is informative at this point. We described earlier that the approach to the first rūpa jhāna disrupts the default attention networks in the brain causing the alpha rhythm characteristic of sensory consciousness to be disrupted into wave-packet-like "spindles", and most meditators with more than 2-3 years of experience showed spindle activity to some degree, indicating some success in disengaging from sensory consciousness.

As meditation progresses, the next EEG feature to develop was the appearance of very slow wave activity, of progressively higher and higher intensity, eventually in some cases to levels unprecedented in any previously published neuroscience studies. In the published paper this was hypothesised to reflect much higher levels of available energy freed as a result of less energy being required to support the previous default sensory networks of brain activity, networks that in effect support our ongoing experience of "I am" and "I do".

The EEG study therefore strongly suggests that the Bojjhaṅgā and jhāna factor Pīti is related to the energy freed following success in establishing the 1st rūpa jhāna, which then in turn corresponds to Pīti being the characterising factor in developing the 2nd rūpa jhāna. For some meditators Pīti expresses itself in outer physical signs such as those mentioned in the Yogāvacara invocation – hairs prickling, bodily vibration or shaking – but even without external signs, meditators in this stage become much more aware of their body, its level of energisation, with an overall sense of being "embodied". This experience of bodily energisation is often accompanied by a sense of exhilaration; not exactly joy, in fact a more physical sensation, but probably why joy came to be used as an approximate translation.

Pīti and Energisation in the EEG

Slow-wave brain activity is familiar in neuroscience during deep nREM (non-rapid eye movement) sleep, also in coma and anaesthesia. But the slow waves during jhāna meditation are very different – more powerful, in some cases more than 1000x stronger than non-meditating resting-state levels; more rhythmic; and also much slower, so much so that in the published study they were termed "Infraslow" waves. The most obvious difference, however, is that meditators are fully conscious, in fact subjectively more intensely "present" than in everyday consciousness.

Figure 4 below shows the EEG of a meditator developing the 2nd rūpa jhāna. This is a 31-electrode recording, with electrode labels listed left (F indicates frontal sites; T, C, P temporal, central

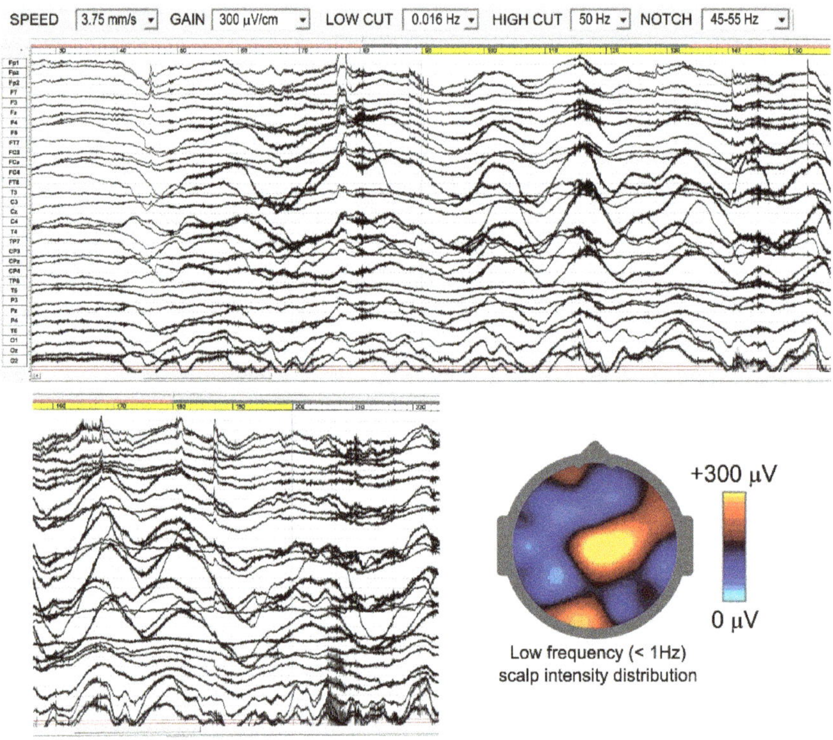

Figure 4 A 200 sec EEG segment showing development of infraslow waves; left to right top, continued below, with scalp intensity map.

and parietal sites; and O occipital sites at the back of the head). The top traces are from the front of the head, those below come from central, temporal and parietal areas moving down across the head, and finally to the bottom traces from the back of the head. The time-scale in seconds is in the top bar. For this meditator, slow waves begin from about 40 secs into meditation, at first rather irregular, but from ~90 secs they become highly rhythmic and very powerful – up to 1000 μV peak-to-peak which equates to 30x resting state levels of ~30 μV, which is an increase in power of 30^2 = ~1000x. That levels of intensity of this magnitude can be deliberately evoked in meditation and sustained with no discomfort for extended periods is completely unprecedented in neuroscience.

Of the 30 subjects recorded in the EEG study, about half showed periods of moderate to strong slow-wave activity during a typically 50-min recording session. Some of these like the example in Figure 4 reaching very high intensity levels. At the same time, all these subjects showed a progressively developing focal region of activity close to the crown of the head, which is illustrated for the subject in Figure 4 by the scalp intensity map at bottom-right.

This intensity map is the average for the segment (90-200 secs) that is yellow-highlighted in the time-bar at the top of Figure 4. The map shows strong focal intensity near the crown of the head, with a mean value (corresponding to the yellow colour in the intensity scale alongside) of more than 300 μV over the 110-sec segment. The development of this vertex or crown of the head focused activity was interpreted in Dennison (2019) as the development of a new vertical axis of jhāna consciousness. It will be seen in the next chapters that this becomes the dominant region of EEG activity in the deeper levels of samādhi in the 3rd and 4th rūpa jhānas.

At the bottom right of the lower panel for this meditator, some instability can be seen, in this case "spike waves". This is a sign that this meditator has not yet fully mastered the tranquilisation of high levels of Pīti into samādhi, which is the function of the 5th Bojjhaṅgā, Passaddhi, to be described in the next chapter.

Embodied

Persons developing the 2nd rūpa jhāna will at some point become highly aware of their bodily systems, whether or not they experience outer signs of strong Pīti. It is as though the body has to "wake up" before becoming able to be incorporated fully into a more complete mind-body integration, or samādhi. Many meditators at this stage find themselves becoming interested in movement exercises in the broad sense; this may include a deeper appreciation of physical activities such as swimming, tennis etc., or more specialised forms like Tai Chi, Chi Gong or Aikido.

Such activities act as forms of "meditation in movement", and together with sitting meditation lead to a deeper understanding of the jhāna term, the "fine material" realm, and how it can be felt in both physical stillness or in physical activity. The outer activities deepen the more internal understandings, and are very helpful in easing persons further forwards on the path to developing the jhānas. And reciprocally, meditators may benefit from a more subtle understanding of how their bodies function, with knock-on effects to more healthy lifestyles.

5 Passaddhi

Tranquilisation, Friday

Thailand, 20th century

This image is specific to the group of seven day-of-birth Buddha Rūpas, and is rarely seen outside that tradition.

Passaddhi is most often translated as tranquillity, and the associated story for this image is of the Buddha, during the 7th week after his enlightenment, reflecting on those who can and cannot be taught, given the extreme subtlety of the Dhamma that he had realised. On this occasion he had accepted his first two lay followers after giving a Dhamma talk, recognising how tranquillity, Passaddhi, can arise in those ready to hear the Dhamma, at the right time, and in particular when the Dhamma is well-taught. What *well-taught* means is an interesting question in its own right; teaching is between two people, and cannot be only one-way for real learning to occur. In the case of meditation this implies *transmission* – what was known formerly by just the teacher, comes to be known by the other person, and there is equality at the moment of shared understanding.

Such moments cannot be forced, and the phrase "right person, right place, right time" is apt. The hands folded at the level of the heart in this Buddha image convey something important at the moment of considering teaching: whether something is recognised between teacher and pupil that can lead to openness and acceptance, allowing the heart to open, to teach. The posture suggests a heart-to-heart transmission based on *metta*, kindness, and ultimately compassion.

If you were born on a Friday you might find yourself reflecting on what Passaddhi means to you, which needs more understanding of Passaddhi in practice since the meaning of tranquilisation can be rather elusive.

Viriya, Pīti and Passaddhi Together

Just as these three Bojjhaṅgās are grouped together in the *Bojjhaṅgā Paritta*, the chanted form of recollection of the seven factors of enlightenment, so too do they appear to be inextricably linked in meditation once a meditator has disengaged to a significant degree from the processes of sensory consciousness. Their interaction, and a meditator's growing understanding of how that works, is key to developing the 2nd rūpa jhāna.

Viriya was described earlier as the driving force for this phase, with Pīti experienced as a kind of awakening of the body, marked by more available energy freed by disengaging from sensory consciousness. The function of Passaddhi appears so intimately connected to how Pīti is experienced that it sometimes seems they must be aspects of the same process. For a meditator it takes time to become familiar with Pīti, how it arises, how it might be maintained, and how it can be calmed, which in a way *defines* the development of the 2nd rūpa jhāna.

Traditionally (as described in the Visuddhimagga for example; Buddhaghosa, 5th century), each of the jhānas can have a fleeting or minor level of development; a middling development; and finally full development, or completion. In the previous chapter, Figure 4, an example was shown of an experienced meditator able to develop with ease very powerful and rhythmic slow waves, with strong development of a crown-of-the-head vertex source in the brain, hypothesised as the new vertical axis of jhāna consciousness. While able to maintain such activity for significant lengths of time, that meditator was still occasionally prone to moments of instability where the energy of Pīti could become unstable. In Figure 4, bottom right, this appears as a brief burst of spike-waves at the back of the head.

Overall, this is probably a person nearing the completion stage of the 2nd rūpa jhāna, on the verge of mastering the process of tranquilising Pīti by the action of Passaddhi. Those negotiating this phase are often unaware of any instability, and may be surprised to see the evidence in their EEG. If instability takes the form of spike-waves, as in the example above, they usually occur in brief bursts of a few seconds at the back of the head.

This kind of activity is usually only seen in neuroscience in cases of absence epilepsy, mostly in children, where the spike-waves are also usually more widespread. In absence epilepsy something happens to disrupt the ongoing sensory consciousness causing a child to lose consciousness for a few minutes, almost like dropping into deep sleep, recovering to be only vaguely aware that something strange had happened; hence the term “absence”.

The spike-waves in meditation are different in detail from those in absence epilepsy (see Dennison, 2019 for a fuller discussion), and the meditator is fully conscious throughout. Based on subjective reports and discussions with meditators showing these phenomena, it seems they relate to the final stages, as a kind of threshold, whereby Pīti and Passaddhi are beginning to harmonise and function together to calm any disturbances in the body allowing a deep mind-body integration to develop, eventually completing the 2nd rūpa jhāna and presaging the more complete samādhi of the 3rd rūpa jhāna.

The categorisation of levels as “fleeting”, middling” and “completion” should not be taken too rigidly as meaning three types of the 2nd rūpa jhāna; or any jhāna for that matter. It may be more the case of attaining jhāna briefly, initially, and only gradually mastering the relevant factors or mental understandings that allow a meditator to extend the duration until, as with the processes of vitakka and vicāra becoming “automatic” in the 1st rūpa jhāna, a meditator learns a degree of mastery of, in this case, Pīti coupled with Passaddhi, in the 2nd rūpa jhāna.

Historical Background: Suppression of Jhāna and Pīti, and Re-emergence

Beginning in the early 1800s, but reaching a crescendo from the mid-1950s, Thailand and Burma were the arena for what have euphemistically been termed “reforms” of Buddhist practices (McCargo, 2012). The reforms were rationalised as embracing

Western scientific ideas, and were also heavily influenced by Christian missionaries who were very active in the education systems of both countries. Those directing the reforms regarded many of the older esoteric practices as corrupt, superstitious or even forms of black magic, and it is likely that some of the outer expressions of Pīti were seen in that light, perhaps even as forms of possession or mental instability, even though such practices were carefully guarded and mostly confined within temples.

Stone mural of ancient Thai life

The most damaging effects of the reforms came in the mid-1950s with heavy political promotion of a "new" vipassanā movement led by the Burmese monk-scholar Mahāsi Sayadaw. He had become the latest figurehead of a line of scholar-monks who believed jhāna meditation was not necessary to complete the Buddhist Path, and that in fact it could be dangerous or for some practitioners an addictive hindrance. New Burmese vipassanā, or "dry" vipassanā ("dry" as in un-moistened by jhāna), quickly gained ground and was adopted by senior and influential figures not only within the Saṅgha, but also in the political and middle classes. In the case of Thailand, temples across the country were instructed to train their monks in the new vipassanā, and to stop teaching and practicing samatha and jhāna meditation.

Nai Boonman, the former monk whose teaching in London and Cambridge from the early 1960s led to the formation of the Samatha Trust, eventually entrusted with carrying on the old samatha and jhāna practices, never spoke openly of this history, and there is only one occasion in this author's memory when he made any direct comment about this background. It was following a big public event at the new Thai Temple in London in either 1965 or 1966, where the opening address was given by a highly political and senior monk brought over from Thailand for the occasion. This person was the figurehead of "new vipassanā" in Thailand, and something dismissive or even contemptuous was said to Nai Boonman either by that monk or one of his attendants. Later that evening, when pressed, Boonman commented that, "within a year, centuries-old practices were destroyed". Which was the reason Boonman had left Thailand and eventually disrobed.

We may never know to what extent those involved in the reforms were simply agents of their times, reflecting larger-scale changes in society that might have occurred in some form or other regardless. Or whether in the larger picture esoteric practices were ripe to be re-expressed and understood in different cultural and wider international contexts. It is also true to say that many persons over the decades have found vipassanā practices helpful as a way-in to meditation, in some cases as a springboard to later practice of ānāpānasati. In the tradition that informs this book, for example, techniques of vipassanā are often used in the early stages to anchor understandings of mindfulness.

Re-emergence

Pīti normally develops naturally at the time meditators begin to detach from sensory consciousness. Around the end of Nai

Boonman's first year teaching in Cambridge, ~1965, a few of his students began to show outward signs of Pīti, even though it had not been named or taught, or his students forewarned. Signs like mild or strong vibration or shaking mostly. Two American students had a hard time; both had been (paid) volunteers in Timothy Leary's LSD experiments at Harvard, and had experienced bad trips with LSD. As a consequence both found the energy of Pīti hard to control, one so bad he would rush out of the room, and eventually he stopped practicing completely. The other was not affected quite so badly, but he was drafted to Vietnam soon after and we never heard what happened to him.

Nai Boonman was greatly intrigued that strong Pīti could arise in Westerners knowing nothing in detail of jhāna meditation. On one occasion he had a meditator demonstrate a form of practice to deliberately arouse very powerful Pīti in front of a few others, but otherwise did not teach the details of such practices openly. As mentioned earlier, Boonman was careful to keep a low profile in his teaching in those early years to avoid censure from the new Thai orthodoxy. He did, however, teach one or two of his students methods to deliberately arouse very high levels of Pīti, instructing them to more openly teach those practices only after he returned to Thailand in 1974.

From 1996, following the success of the Samatha Trust in establishing a national meditation centre in Wales, Nai Boonman began to visit the UK annually for short periods to continue teaching, and from around 2006 adopted a more open approach in asking experienced meditators to demonstrate the deliberate arousal of strong Pīti in front of the larger group on intensive retreats. These were remarkable occasions, with a wide range of manifestations of powerful Pīti, which Boonman allowed to take their course with no attempt to comment, analyse, control or explain the different manifestations.

Many meditators benefited greatly in their own meditation

practice from either being the person to demonstrate, or through witnessing demonstrations by others. Some, however, found the demonstrations unsettling, so much so for some that they ceased practicing, at least for a while. In retrospect, I believe this was a glimpse into how Pīti might have been seen as problematic during the "reforms" in Southeast Asian Buddhist countries.

Pīti and Passaddhi in the EEG

Some meditators develop Pīti without strong physical manifestations and are often surprised to see the evidence in their EEG, such as strong slow waves, spike-waves or other instabilities. The practice of *deliberately* choosing to develop Pīti more strongly is partly to experience just how powerful the deeper stages of meditation can become, which is not always appreciated by those schools of practice that regard samatha meditation as simply a state of calm and tranquillity.

In fact the Pāli term jhāna has two roots: the more familiar *jhāyati* translated as "meditation" or "concentration"; but a second root *jhāpeti* meaning "to burn up", usually taken to mean burning up the hindrances. In this sense jhāna is far from a passive state; behind the immense stillness of deep absorption is considerable power as will become clear in the next chapters, and in the historic jhāna traditions the 4th rūpa jhāna is regarded as the gateway to a variety of psychic powers, the *abhiññās*.

A second benefit for practicing the deliberate arousal of strong Pīti is that it necessarily requires meditators to learn-by-doing how to calm down, tranquilise or incorporate the energy of Pīti into deeper stages of absorption. It can be helpful in understanding the subtle arousal of Pīti, but more importantly the delicacy of the processes of its tranquilisation. The practices of deliberate arousal were carefully protected in the oral traditions of the Yogāvacara, and have been variously called one-way practice, psychic-power practice, or simply Pīti practice; they are also similar to vase-breathing or *Tummo* in Tibetan yoga. Figure 5 is a "historic", picture, the first recording in 2010 of a meditator arousing a brief (~4 secs) but strong burst of Pīti.

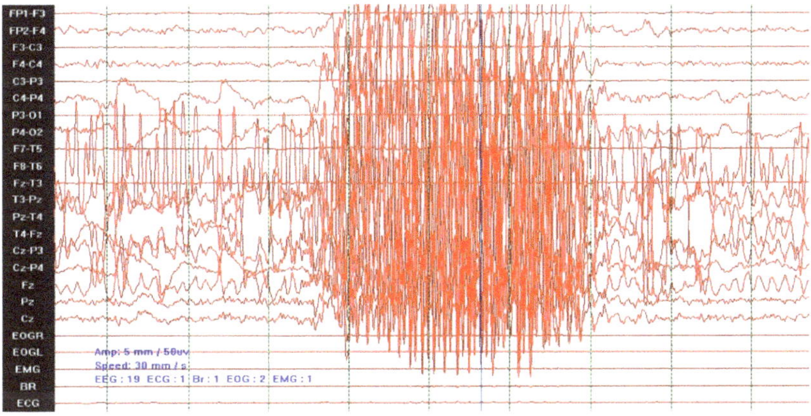

Figure 5 An early recording of Pīti in 2010.

Those early recordings were very prone to contamination between movement artifacts (shaking of the headcap connecting wires) and brain activity, and it was not until more sophisticated equipment was acquired from 2014 onwards that the brain activity proper could be distinguished in more detail.

Figure 6 below is from Dennison (2019) and shows two examples. The top two panels are from a meditator, **A**, very experienced in this practice, and able to moderate the seizure-like effects such that the details of brain activity can still be analysed. The first sign of increasing energization is the development of occipital spike waves (far left, bottom traces), followed over the next 7 secs by three very brief global spasms or bursts, before the main body of the "seizure" ~15 secs later, lasting about 70 secs. Physically, the meditator shows mild clonic jerks (a term used in epilepsy studies to describe the outer physical signs in grand-mal epilepsy), or bodily vibration, mainly along a vertical bodily axis.

The expanded view below the top panel shows the occipital activity at the back of the head in more detail. This includes spike waves, together with a related and near-perfect sinusoidal rhythm at the right temporal site T6, reaching remarkable intensities ~3000 μV peak-to-peak, a 10,000x increase in power compared to the resting state.

The head plots (seen from above) at right show the two

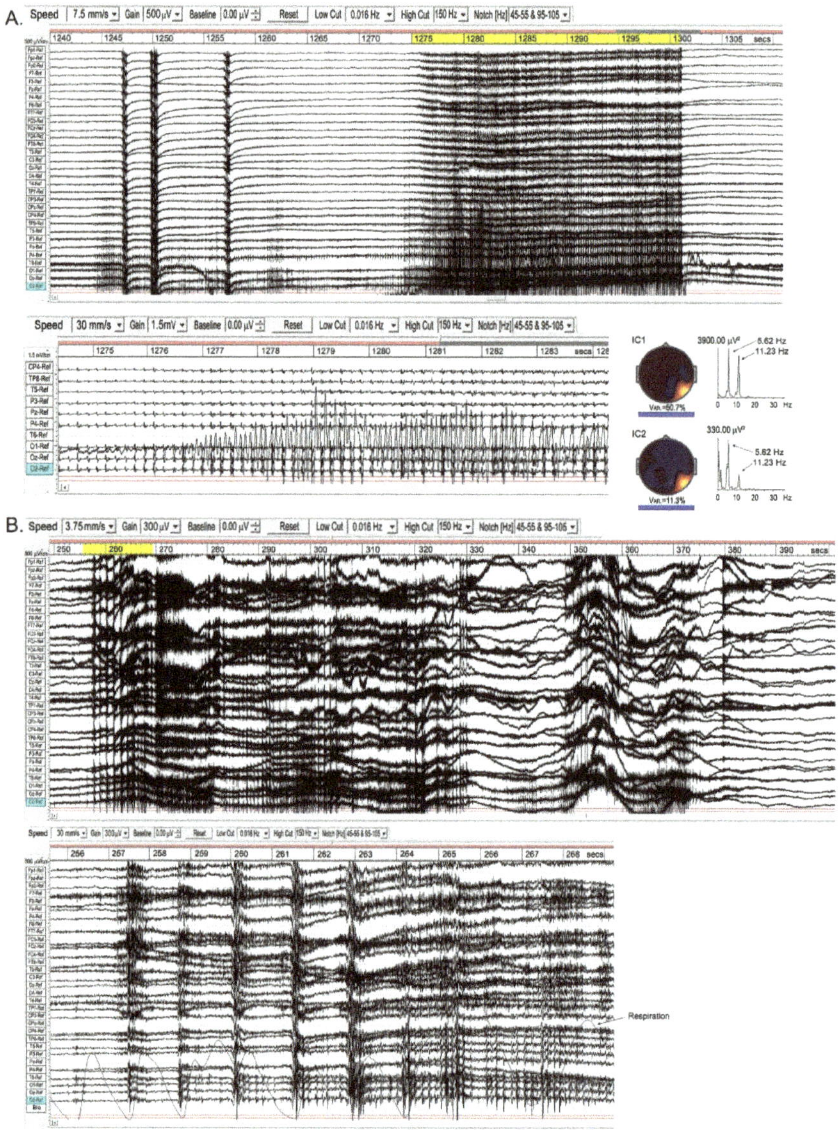

Figure 6 Deliberate arousal of Pīti. Two examples: **A.** 2018; **B.** 2015.

strongest underlying cortical sources taken from an eLoreta analysis of the yellow-highlighted segment (eLoreta is a rather beautiful mathematical algorithm that transforms surface EEG activity via a "reverse solution" to reveal the underlying deeper cortical brain sources driving the surface scalp activity).

These sources are highly localised in the right-hand medial temporal gyrus (scalp site T6); the spike-wave frequency is 5.62 Hz and the temporal rhythm is at the first harmonic 11.23 Hz. It will remain for other researchers to pursue the possible significance of these observations to understanding the underlying mechanisms of epilepsy.

Subject **B** in the two lower panels of Figure 6 shows a more complex recording of a 150-sec episode with the early (yellow-highlighted) portion expanded in the bottom panel. The EEG again shows brief spasms or bursts at onset, shown in the expanded view below, together with the rhythmic trace of respiration low down. Although these bursts coincide with the end of out-breaths, the breathing rhythm is not disturbed until the development of the paroxysmal effects is well-underway, and we do not believe that the processes of hypercapnia/hypocapnia (abnormally disturbed levels of carbon dioxide in the blood) play a role as they can in the onset of epilepsy in sleep.

In this case, occipital spike waves develop progressively rather than precede the "seizure" as in example A. Because this example is more complex, with much stronger clonic (physical movement) activity as well as spike-waves and strong infra-slow-wave (ISW) bursts, and complex higher frequency activity extending into the gamma band, a source analysis proved inconclusive in identifying deeper brain sources.

Strong infraslow waves, as in this example, often feature in the more clonic examples of this kind of intense Pīti. It is likely they perform a containment function for the disturbance, related to their much longer and slower time-scale, which allows meditators to remain mentally undisturbed during the practice.

Some interest has been shown among epilepsy researchers as to whether some of the basic features of this form of meditation might be of use to chronic epilepsy sufferers to moderate seizure frequency. It is likely that the long and detailed development of attention may be the key factor that allows experienced meditators to perform this practice with no discomfort.

Some Final Thoughts on Pīti

Any samatha meditators reading this chapter should not be too concerned if they do not experience strong outer signs of Pīti; some meditators, for example, show it in their EEG and are unaware of it, except for a strong sense of feeling embodied. And there may also be a group of meditators who are able to establish strong body-mind integration without the need for strong expressions of Pīti. After performing recordings of a wide range of meditators, both male and female, the author is left with the impression that natural variations in peoples' nervous system structures play a role, and that neither is there a gender distinction in this ability.

It should also be said that some (few) meditators overvalue being able to arouse high levels of Pīti, and for a while may become too attached to that ability. This may also have been a factor in the criticisms of samatha and jhāna meditation in the 1950s' reform movements. If left at that high level, strong expressions of Pīti alone will not lead to jhāna until the meditator learns how to master it by Passaddhi, and to recognise the far greater value in being able to do so.

Although jhāna practice has shown something of a slow resurgence since the 1980s/1990s, the "new" versions are post-reform understandings of jhāna, where the role of Pīti seems to have been lost, or at least not fully understood.

6 Samādhi

Absorption, Yoga, Saturday

Phra Nak Prok, Thailand mid-20th century

The Buddha image for Samādhi, and for Saturday, is Phra Nak Prok, the "Buddha protected by the Naga King"; sometimes shown with seven heads, sometimes nine. The example on the previous page is beautifully detailed in silver, but not very old, perhaps around 100 years. A second example below is from a cave temple in Phetchaburi Province, Thailand, 150-200 kms Southwest of Bangkok, believed to be early 20th century but possibly older since many Buddha images in caves are heavily restored versions of much older images.

The story for this image relates to the seven weeks following the Buddha's enlightenment that he spent under or near to the Bodhi tree. In the last chapter, Passaddhi was related to the seven days contemplating the great subtlety of the Dhamma, whether and how to teach, and how Passaddhi can arise after hearing Dhamma well-taught.

At the end of those seven days the Buddha moved to practice under another tree just south of the Bodhi tree, where he entered Samādhi for a further seven days sheltered by a Nāga king.

Samādhi is often translated as concentration, but when it comes to developing jhāna it is much more than that. It derives from two roots, *sama*, together, and *dhā*, to place; meaning placing or bringing together. So at the point of establishing Samādhi, everything begins to come together, and in its full development nothing is left out. The two consecutive events in the stories of the Buddha's enlightenment that correspond to the two Bojjhaṅgās, Passaddhi and Samādhi, match exactly the progression in meditation as to how Samādhi develops as a direct result of the integration and harmony between Pīti and Passaddhi.

The discussion in the previous chapter, supported by the EEG study, describes a close inter-relationship between Pīti and Passaddhi as a meditator develops the 2nd rūpa jhāna, until eventually they work in harmony as bodily disturbances fade, and residual traces of instability in the EEG disappear.

Just as vitakka and vicāra do not disappear at completion of the 1st rūpa jhāna, neither does Pīti disappear at completion of the 2nd rūpa jhāna. In the subtle harmony of Pīti and Passaddhi working together, the bodily energies represented by Pīti become incorporated into a body-mind Samādhi imbued with great latent power. This process is a description of *Yoga*, hence the term Yogāvacara for those who follow the path of developing the jhānas. Rather than try to translate the word Samādhi, we retain it as it is.

If Pīti is understood, developed and then tranquilised fully by the quality of Passaddhi, the 2nd rūpa jhāna becomes complete and the 3rd rūpa jhāna emerges. The subjective experience is then indeed that "nothing is left out". In some Buddhist texts such as the Visuddhimagga or Vimuttimagga, this is also described as the meditator becoming fully conscious; for the first time if it is the first experience of the 3rd rūpa jhāna. "Fully conscious" and "nothing left out" are equivalent; no trace remains of possible distraction, no trace remains of an object of consciousness other than the absorption and stillness of jhāna, and the closest description of the now fully developed jhāna consciousness is of being fully "present"; an embodied presence.

Samādhi in the EEG and the Emergence of Jhāna Consciousness

In Figure 4 (Chapter 4), an example was shown of a meditator able to maintain strong rhythmic slow waves consistently, with only occasional disruption by untranquilised Pīti, which was interpreted as nearing completion of the 2nd rūpa jhāna. Figure 4 also showed strong development of a crown-of-the-head vertex focus of brain activity. Figure 7 below shows brain activity in the form of 3D cortical sources averaged across a group of experienced meditators negotiating development from the 1st to the 2nd rūpa jhāna.

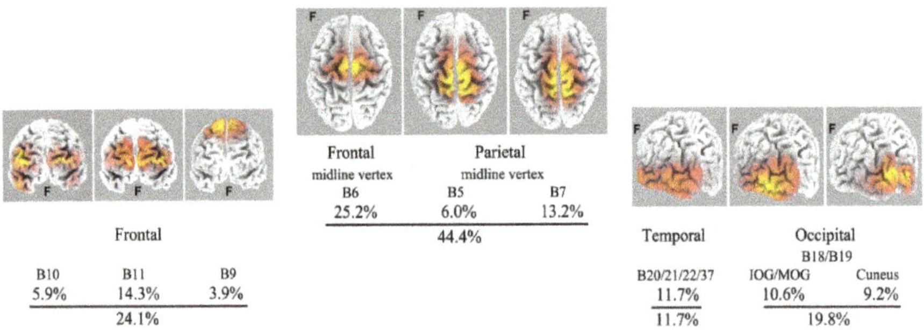

Figure 7 Three-dimensional plots of brain activity showing regions of interest (ROIs) and their neuroscience Brodmann-site labels (B5, 6, 7 etc.) activated during jhāna meditation.

The strongest activity was around the crown of the head for this group of meditators, bridging the frontal-parietal divide, and amounting to 44.4% of the total activity across the group. The remainder activity was distributed between frontal regions (24.1%), and posterior/temporal regions (19.8%/11.7%). In Dennison (2019) the posterior-frontal regions of interest were hypothesised to represent subject-object poles of consciousness; the posterior visual cortex as the "I/Eye" subject position, and the frontal cortex normally specialised in executive/cognitive functions the object position.

However, this does not mean that these meditators were falling back into crudely cognitive sensory consciousness between moments of touching jhāna. The activity across the head for all these meditators was already becoming dominated by infraslow-wave activity (~0.05-0.1 Hz), quite different to the alpha (~10 Hz) and beta (18-25 Hz) rhythms characteristic of cognitive processing. However, until the 1st rūpa jhāna is mastered, it is as though the previous networks of sensory consciousness are still present as a "shadow", sometimes described in Buddhist texts as the "near enemy" of jhāna consciousness, which in these distributions is represented by the emerging and eventually dominant crown-of-head ROI.

These averaged distributions should also not be interpreted that all ROIs are active as a mix at the same time for individual meditators; rather they represent some meditators able to maintain jhāna for longer periods than others. Figure 8 below is an example of how experience can develop and deepen for a meditator over 2-3 years of practice.

The upper panel in Figure 8 is part of a recording made in 2014, showing very strong infraslow waves. The inset intensity map corresponds to the yellow-highlighted segment and shows an intense hot-spot just posterior to the vertex, with surrounding areas at very low levels of intensity mostly at left-frontal and left-posterior areas.

Three years later (lower panel), with more experience, the activity is now heavily dominated by infraslow waves near and slightly posterior to the crown of the head, and the inset intensity map shows that apart from the crown focal activity, all other brain networks are almost totally quiet. To get an idea of just how much of the brain's activity is now focused at the crown of the head, a detailed analysis of all possible underlying cortical sources was carried out for 600-sec samples from each of the two years, and the comparison is shown in Figure 9.

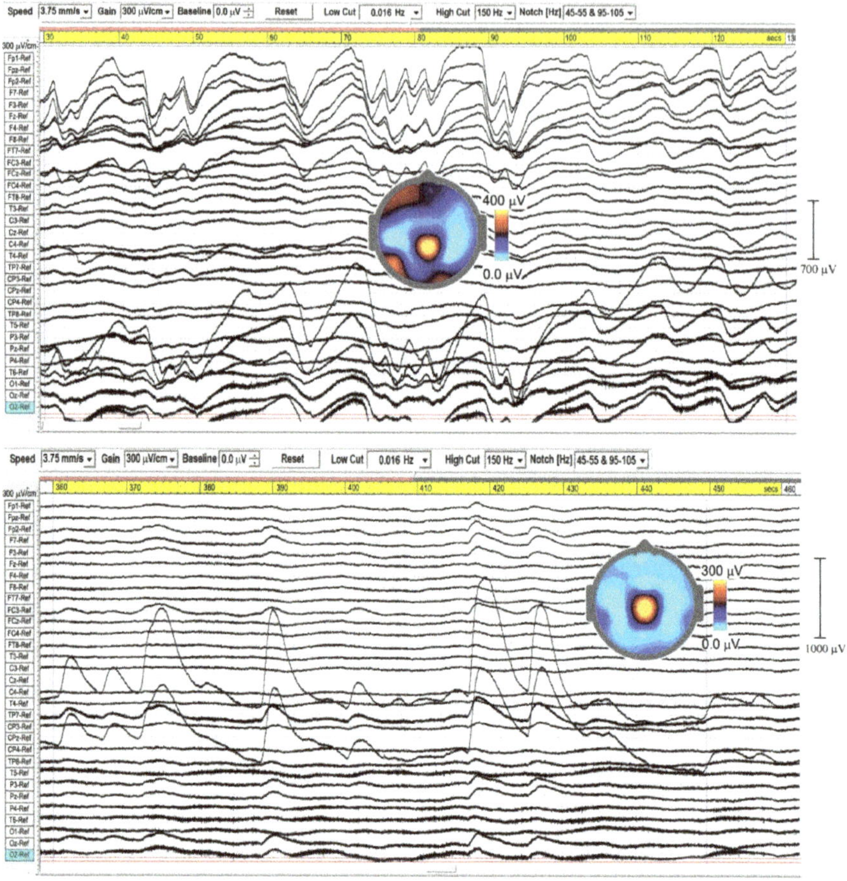

Figure 8 Development of Samādhi for a meditator recorded in 2014 and, with more experience, in 2017.

The comparison is of two 600-sec segments across the full frequency range to capture all activity from infraslow 0.016 Hz up to the high gamma frequencies 150 Hz. Using an eLoreta analysis mentioned earlier, the percentage contributions of all possible underlying cortical brain sources were calculated. In 2014, 92.8% of the total brain electrical activity was focused near the vertex, and in 2017 this had increased to an astonishing 99.7%. These figures can be compared to the subject shown earlier in Figure 4, where the percentage at the vertex varied during the recording from 70-85%, the higher figure coming from the most consistently maintained strong infraslow waves.

Meditator recorded in 2014, 2017; 600 sec segments, 0.016-150 Hz
ROIs as % of total signals' variance across all 31 ind. cmpts.

2014		2017
5.7%	Frontal B11 B47 SFG MFG IFG	0.2%
92.8%	Vertex Fronto-parietal B4 B5 B6 B7 MFG SFG PCL PCG	99.7%
1.5%	Occipital B18 B19 Cun MOG	0.1%

Figure 9 Degree of focus at the crown of the head vertex.

Samādhi: Stages, or Depth

The percentages of activity near the crown of the head describe a process of development of a new vertical axis in the brain which appears to be unique to this form of jhāna meditation, with no precedent in neuroscience. From our discussion so far, we believe we are seeing evidence of how jhāna consciousness develops progressively in the 2nd, 3rd and 4th rūpa jhānas.

When the percentage activity at the crown of the head exceeds 90% and in the one example above over 99%, we are reminded of the description of Samādhi in the 3rd and 4th rūpa jhānas as "nothing is left out". It is as though the energy implicit within all the previously complex distributed activity in the brain, in all the networks supporting our everyday sensory consciousness, in other words all that activity that supports and maintains the continuity of "I am" and "I do", becomes available and is drawn into this new and highly focused vertical axis.

From the second jhāna onwards, meditators subjectively describe their experience as embodied presence, rather than the more usual everyday consciousness of "something", and this comes to completion in the 3rd and 4th rūpa jhānas. The Samādhi at this stage is far removed from sensory consciousness processes of naming, recognition or comparison, and equally free from notions of time and space. Without such ordering in time and space, including conventional language of subject-verb-object we would lose the continuity of "I am" and "I do". At this point the notion of developing the jhānas in stages, of "getting anywhere", of 2nd to 3rd to 4th becomes far too crude.

Once a meditator has sufficient experience of the 2nd and 3rd rūpa jhānas, even if not yet perfect, it is possible to let go entirely of the idea of stages and simply allow the stillness of jhāna to deepen, and deepen more. The all-encompassing peace, stillness and clarity constitute the sense of presence, and the stillness alone as the "signature" of jhāna is sufficient to lead the meditator into complete absorption. However, this requires a sophisticated understanding of mindfulness, Sati, since if Sati lapses the practice will revert, sooner rather than later, to one of the earlier stages, or even back to sensory consciousness.

The kind of Sati required needs to be increasingly subtle to match the stillness; and in fact both go together. If the breath is allowed to follow a natural process of becoming increasingly fine, so not to disturb the stillness, eventually everything comes to a still point of what might be called "un-breath", rather than in- and out-breath, in the 4th rūpa jhāna. In the Yogāvacara tradition, this is likened to the breath of the foetus in the womb.

An Observer Effect?

An important point should be noted about recording EEG brain activity of meditators. Several meditators commented they were not able to go as far as they might in their usual individual practice at home, or on retreats, due to a subtle self-consciousness due to being recorded. In fact it is no mean achievement to do as well as so many of the subjects managed to do, and this question highlights something that is reminiscent of the "observer effect" in quantum physics, where as soon as anything is observed, it is changed or disrupted to some degree.

This makes it difficult to imagine developing to completion the extremely fine balance of the 4th rūpa jhāna while being recorded, to say nothing of the difficulty of recording the arūpa or formless jhānas.

Re-collection

In becoming familiar with the higher jhānas, it is necessary to find another way of understanding beyond the crude naming of conventional language. In the oral Yogāvacara tradition the notion of the fine-material sphere parallels a little-used term of "twilight language" (Bucknell, R. and Stuart-Fox, M, 1986). At the end of a meditation practice, for example, it is recommended that the meditator remains with the experience of stillness without moving, or yet opening his/her eyes for a while. This is the practice of Recollection, already mentioned briefly in Chapter 3, but not the kind of recollection based on language in an attempt to verbally recollect what has been experienced, and how it was done.

For example, if the meditator had been deeply absorbed in the samādhi of the 3rd rūpa jhāna, the stillness at the end of practice would have a deeply blissful and satisfying quality (sukha), which may last for a considerable time. After some time, however, it will fade to be replaced by a still deeply satisfying peace, but one where the body in particular is experienced as being totally at peace, as in the 2nd rūpa jhāna. Again after some time the meditator will become aware of the pull to "attend"; the pull towards the processes of vitakka and vicāra of the 1st rūpa jhāna. And finally he or she will return quite naturally to full sensory consciousness.

In this way meditators come to know "where they have been", and gradually develop a deeper understanding of the jhāna factors based on direct experience rather than words. Which then makes it possible to recollect the qualities of any particular jhāna, and eventually to become able to simply "go there". In the oral tradition of developing mastery of jhāna, and in the Yogāvacara, this ability is perfected by the practice of moving through the jhānas in forward or reverse order, or jumping or changing the order until the jhānas are fully understood by *feel* and direct experience rather than by labels or words.

Jhāna Consciousness

It is important to understand that throughout all the jhānas, including the formless arūpa jhānas, although we are not dealing with them in this book, meditators never lose consciousness. Yet by definition consciousness has to have an object, to be conscious *of*. So what then is the equivalent in jhāna consciousness, where subjectively meditators describe the experience as an almost timeless "presence"?

Two views have been expressed on this. One is that each moment of consciousness becomes the object of the next, giving the illusion of perfectly still and continuous undisturbed consciousness. Which would also correspond to the much longer 10-60 secs time scale-factor of jhāna compared to the ~100 msec of sensory consciousness, based on the EEG study. This is envisaged as a high-level and very fast process, a kind of unconscious flickering, and we might wonder at the role of background very fast gamma activity (40-150 Hz), albeit very weak, and brief gamma bursts that are observed in the EEG recordings (Dennison, 2019).

Such a very fast reflexive process might also correspond, in the quite different terminology of mathematical neuroscience, to a highly stable state of reciprocal top-down–bottom-up recurrent processing (Friston *et al.*, 2016) where the error between prediction and current state has been reduced to effectively zero, at least for a while.

A second view is that the body itself becomes the supporting object of jhāna consciousness, as part of a deep brain-body metabolic integration. It may be relevant that a recent paper in a leading neuroscience journal (Solms, 2019) has argued that the upper-brain stem, the intermediary region in our model between cortical brain processes and bodily systems, may be a more likely site for core processes of consciousness than the larger brain cortex.

The role of the body is certainly well-recognised in ancient Buddhist texts, particularly in the evocative and intriguing term "Body Witness" (káyasakkhin, Pāli) found in Buddhaghosa's 5th century Visuddhimagga, Path of Purification. This term is reserved for those who attain the Path of Realisation after completing the four rūpa jhānas; which in our discussion reflects the full development of mind-body samādhi, or Yoga.

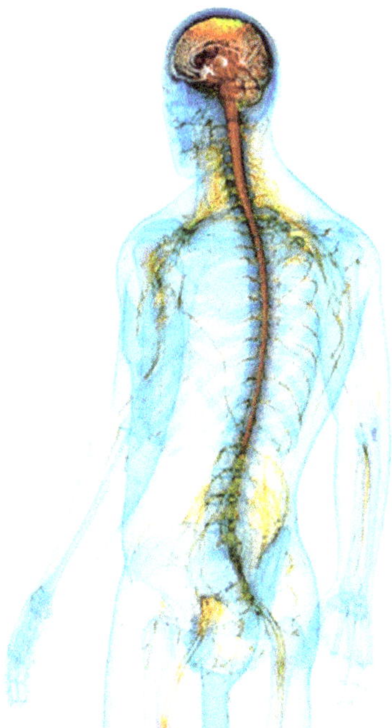

Figure 10 The brain-body axis.

Figure 10 is a conceptual illustration of the hypothesised brain-body axis of jhāna consciousness. What we have termed the vertex region of interest (ROI), the area of cortex near the crown of the head, is well-known in neuroscience to have high connectivity down through core regions of the brain into the brain stem, and from there into the Vagus networks of the sympathetic and parasympathetic systems of the body.

Although yet unpublished, measurements of the heart-rate variability (HRV) of meditators practising this form of meditation, before and during, show an almost doubling of HRV in meditation indicating a shift towards the deeply integrative para-sympathetic nervous system mode rather than the “readiness for action” characteristics of the sympathetic system.

7 Upekkhā

Equanimity, Sunday

Thailand, mid-20th century

The Buddha image for Upekkhā relates to the 2nd week after his enlightenment, when the Buddha rose from meditation under the Bodhi tree to move some distance away where he stood for a further seven days gazing at the Bodhi tree – it is said "with unwavering gaze, eyes open and never blinking". This example is solid bronze, about 20 inches tall, and was originally gilded but only traces remain in the folds of the robe. Its eyes are formed of mother of pearl and a black stone, probably onyx, although tektite was used for some much older images. This one is believed to be about 150 years old.

Almost nothing is written of this day-of-the-week Buddha image tradition, and it is only in writing this book that this author has more fully realised the intriguing subtlety of how both the stories behind the choice of image, together with the forms, postures and mudras of the images, *together* illuminate the meanings of the particular Bojjhaṅgās .

So in this case what does the form of this image convey?

- The overall posture is standing, erect, firm but relaxed, with the hands placed together at rest, not performing any particular function. The overall impression is of "composure"; and the dictionary definition of composure is "calm, tranquil, free from disturbance or agitation", which is a good starting point towards understanding Upekkhā. Standing erect is also what as human beings we have evolved to do; it is quintessentially "human", and in this case reminds us that what was realised by the Buddha began as the journey of a normal human being, in this case a man.
- Second, the very specific description of "open eyes, unblinking, with unwavering gaze". Now while blinking is well-understood as necessary to keep the corneas of the eyes moist, less well-known is that blinking is strongly related to cognitive processing. In a similar way that heart-rate variability (HRV), mentioned in the previous chapter, is a

measure of the degree of stress or ease in the body, a similar measure of blink-rate variability (BRV), also the strength of blinking, is related to the degree of cognitive processing, and its level of complexity. In the EEG study, for example, the effects of eye blinks on frontal electrodes gradually become less and less frequent, and less intense, as meditation develops. So the description of steady gaze without blinking might well be a measure of the Buddha's Upekkhā, detached from cognitive processing, maintained for those seven days.

In the previous chapter it was mentioned that a person's normal sense of time changes in jhāna meditation. In everyday consciousness an orderly progression in time, both physically and mentally, is essential to give continuity to the experience of "I am" and "I do", but this becomes more fluid as meditation deepens. In Chapter 1 it was remarked that the first step to establish mindfulness, Sati, aa a moment in time and space, also establishes a potential completion in the future.

Nai Boonman once asked a group of meditators whether, if they really understood where meditation might lead them, and what it might incur, would they have started meditation at all? A bit later he added, "And what if you come to a point where to go forward, you know at the same time there will be no going back. While also at the same time you have no idea of what going forwards might mean?"

On a completely different level, the moment of a birth instantly establishes that a death will occur at some point in the future; and if you are of a "kamma" inclination, that is, have the belief in a continuity of lives, then the reverse too, that a death will inevitably lead to a rebirth. And how is it that only in old age do we begin to understand our journey up to that point, often including vivid memories of the far past, even as short-term memory becomes erratic.

Not unrelated, also, is the practice of staying with the stillness at the end of meditation, as a form of re-collection, described in the previous chapter. And how non-cognitively the stillness leads to direct understanding of where we have been, which jhāna, and the subtleties of how it all unfolded.

So the form of the Sunday Buddha image and the context of the story, gazing unwaveringly at the Bodhi tree where he had completed his journey, becomes an image of understanding all that had gone before, the full understanding of enlightenment and the Path to enlightenment. In this sense, Upekkhā is an expression of enlightenment itself, far more than the commonly-used translation tranquillity, which is the reason we retain the word Upekkhā, as we did Samādhi, rather than try to translate it at all.

All That Has Gone Before

In the context of this book, all that has gone before are the first six Bojjhaṅgās, now completed in Upekkhā in this final chapter. Their relationship to the jhānas is summarised in Figure 11 below, together with the factors of the Buddhist Eightfold Path.

- In the left-hand column, mindfulness and concentration are often taught as the minimum starting points to develop meditation; this was the approach of Nai Boonman starting to teach in the UK in the 1960s.
- In the second column, starting at the top, the first two Bojjhaṅgās, Sati and Dhamma-vicaya, develop and redirect attention, and in the language of jhāna develop the first two jhāna factors, vitakka and vicāra. Vitakka and vicāra are progressively perfected as the 1st rūpa jhāna develops (third column); and the fulfilment of the 1st rūpa jhāna signals temporary disengagement from sensory consciousness.

  At this point, Pīti and sukha are present, although far from fully developed, and it is vitakka and vicāra that "hold" the 1st rūpa jhāna.

Samatha-Vipassanā	The Bojjhaṅgās Factors of Enlightenment	Jhānas and Rūpa Jhāna (RJ) Factors RJ1	RJ2	RJ3	RJ4	Eightfold Path Factors
	Sati Mindfulness	**Vitakka**	(Vitakka)	(Vitakka)	(Vitakka)	Division of Paññā **Sammā Diṭṭhi** Right view
	Dhamma-vicaya Investigation	**Vicāra**	(Vicāra)	(Vicāra)	(Vicāra)	**Sammā Sankappa** Right intention
Mindfulness ↑ **Concentration**	**Viriya** Vigour					Division of Sīla **Sammā Vācā** Right speech
	Pīti Energisation ("joy")	Pīti	**Pīti**	(Pīti)	(Pīti)	**Sammā Kammanta** Right action
	Passaddhi Tranquilisation	Sukha	Sukha	**Sukha**	(Sukha)	**Sammā Ājiva** Right livelihood
	Samādhi Concentration/ Absorption	(Ekagattā)	(Ekagattā)	**Samādhi**		Division of Samādhi **Sammā Vāyāma** Right effort
	Upekkhā Equanimity				**Upekkhā**	**Sammā Sati** Right mindfulness **Sammā Samādhi** Right concentration

Figure 11 The Bojjhaṅgās, Jhānas and Eightfold Path.

- When vitakka and vicāra are sufficiently mastered they become automatic, and they become the foundations or supports (= bracketed) for the new "vihāra" or dwelling for the 2nd and higher jhānas. Viriya, Pīti and Passaddhi now become freed to develop. Pīti is the characterising focus of the 2nd rūpa jhāna (fourth column), and the development of the 2nd jhāna is a progressive integration and harmonisation of Viriya, Pīti and Passaddhi.
- When Pīti becomes fully incorporated with Viriya and Passaddhi into the developing Samādhi, it in turn becomes part of the foundations for the 3rd rūpa jhāna (column 5). With no more disturbance in the body, which equates to no more thinking, naming or any wish for orientation in time and space,

what remains is simply deep peace and happiness, *sukha*, subjectively experienced as being completely conscious with nothing left out. Samadhi is now fully developed, which together with sukha constitutes the 3rd rūpa jhāna.

- As familiarity with the 3rd jhāna develops, the balance of the two factors sukha and Samādhi changes, such that the subtle disturbance of happiness, rooted in subtle attachment and the need for positive feeling leads to it being progressively let go, until only Samādhi remains, which is now so all-encompassing and characterised by no dependence on feeling, neither feeling nor not feeling, that the 4th rūpa jhāna emerges or is attained and for which the term Upekkhā rather than Samādhi is now appropriate (sixth column).
- The seventh column lists the factors of the Noble Eightfold Path. This is not exactly a practice-related structure in the same sense that the Bojjhaṅgās and jhānas are, but is closely related and describes the structure of a life well-lived, and which can be consistent with developing all the qualities described by the Bojjhaṅgās and the jhānas. Readers may wish to make their own associations between the different factors and categories.

In the oral tradition, it is also said that full development of each of the rūpa jhānas, the 1st, 2nd, 3rd and 4th, equates to a temporary experience of the four stages of the Path to Enlightenment, and those who experience those stages – stream entry (Sotāpanna), once-return (Sakadāgāmin), non-return (Anāgāmin), and Arahat (fully realised) – respectively.

The Limits of Language and Structure

Lists and structures such as these can be helpful as an initial orientation, but the cognitive processes involved in giving attention to or thinking about the ideas and categories they contain need to be put to one side when actually starting meditation. In developing the 1st rūpa jhāna, this is achieved first by re-directing attention to the object of meditation, usually the breath, rather than sensory input, and to then develop and become familiar with the processes of vitakka and vicāra as described in Chapters 1 and 2.

As the higher jhānas become increasingly separated from sensory consciousness, meditators become less dependent on words for orientation, and more aware of the fine-material realm of jhāna, and more able to appreciate the symbolic level and metaphor. Structures such as the Bojjhaṅgās become part of "all that has gone before", and to some extent become part of invocation, mentioned earlier in Chapter 3.

At this level, the crude sense of time and space eases, and the factors, whether of the Bojjhaṅgās or the jhānas, can appear to arise together, or are no longer experienced as concrete separate words with fixed meanings as ordinary language starts to fail. Ideas of "stages" or "levels" are inadequate, and fade as absorption deepens into Samādhi and eventually Upekkhā.

The Yogāvacara

The ancient tradition of the Yogāvacara uses structure only in small doses, and instead makes wide use of metaphor, a twilight language of syllables and mantra, and evocative diagrams or *yantra*, often coupled with syllables or characters. An example is the concept of developing or building a Dhammakāya body in meditation; a body of Dhamma that in some sense replaces a person's birth body, at least temporarily. (Somewhat related is the practice in Buddhist countries of a mother whose son ordains as a monk, being the one to offer him a monk's alms-bowl, symbolic of a new womb for his new life.)

Figure 12 is an example of a class of yantra known as "Ong Phra Yan", where Ong Phra means the body of the Buddha, or body of a monk. Yantras are drawn in one movement, usually on the out-breath, while maintaining Sati and Dhamma-vicaya, and ideally from a mental stance of upacāra samādhi, the threshold of jhāna. To execute a yantra is an act of samatha, to grasp its meaning is vipassanā.

Figure 12 Yan Ong Phra

This example is accompanied by the characters MA A U, written in the ancient Cambodian *khom* script and placed progressively upwards in the drawing. MA, sounded low down in the abdomen and diaphragm, is the foundation, the mother; also the invocation of "all that has gone before". A, the shortest vowel sounded at the back of the throat, has the power to "cut", or negate: placed in front of a Pāli word it transforms, for example rūpa, form, to arūpa, formless; or atta, self to anatta, no-self. In meditation it represents the "cut" of consciousness or change of lineage that a meditator experiences in the transition from sensory consciousness to jhāna consciousness; or the change of lineage from the mundane world of experience to the supramundane Path.

In Pāli, the character U in front of a word adds the sense of "upwards", or "higher": as in pāramī, perfection, and upapāramī higher perfection; or sampadā, blessing, and upasampadā, higher blessing (in Buddhist countries, Upasampadā is also used to designate a monk's higher or full ordination). In the Ong Phra yantra it denotes the rising-up, freed from sensory consciousness, when someone attains jhāna, or the Path.

Executing yantra is often performed in combination with meditation as an alternative approach in the spirit of the "fine-material", or the level of subtle form. A meditator might carry over the experience of drawing an Ong Phra yantra into a parallel feeling in meditation of drawing together all the systems of mind and body towards an ever-deeper absorption, while attending to the in- and out-breaths and their movements in the body, in the same manner as the stroke of the pen in drawing the yantra.

Just as drawing a yantra is rarely perfect the first time, each meditation sitting may also be imperfect. With each repetition, however, something is added, understanding and skill gradually grow. In the case of the yantra, the drawing becomes "empowered", by Pīti via the person who executes it, while for the meditator the Dhammakāya body becomes more clearly defined, and the experience of jhāna matures.

References

Bizot, F. (1992) Le Chemin de Lanka. Paris: l'École française d'Extrême-Orient, 101-27.

Brahmāli (2007) Jhāna and Lokuttara-jhāna. *Buddhist Studies Review*, **24**(1), 75-90.

Bucknell, R. and Stuart-Fox, M. (1986) *The Twilight Language: Explorations in Buddhist Language and Symbolism*. London: Curzon Press.

Buddhaghosa (5th century) *The Path of Purification: Visuddhimagga*. Kandy, Sri Lanka: Buddhist Publication Society, 2011.

Dennison, P.A. (2019) The human default consciousness and its disruption: insights from an EEG study of Buddhist jhāna meditation. *Front. Hum. Neurosci.* 13: 178. doi: 10.3389/fnhum.2019.00178

McCargo, D. (2012) The changing politics of Thailand's Buddhist order. *Critical Asian Studies*, **44**(4), 627-42. doi: 10.1080/14672715.2012.738544

Milner, A.D. (2017) How do the two visual streams interact with each other? *Exp. Brain Res.* 235(5): 1297-1308. doi: 10.1007/s00221-017-4917-4

Petersen, S.E. and Posner, M.I. (2012) The attention system of the brain: 20 years after. *Annu. Rev. Neurosci.* 35: 73-89. doi: 10.1146/annurev-neuro-062111-150-525

Rhys Davids T.W. (ed.) (1896) *The Yogavacara's Manual*. London: Pali Text Society.

Seth, A.K. and Friston, K.J. (2016) Active interoceptive inference and the emotional brain. *Phil. Trans. R. Soc.* B 371: 20160007. doi: 10.1098/rstb.2016.0007

Solms, M. (2019) The hard problem of consciousness and the free energy principle. Front. Psych. 9:2714. doi: 10.3389/fpsyg.2018.02714

Thich Nhat Hanh (2008) *Breathe, You Are Alive: The Sutra on the Full Awareness of Breathing*. New York: Parallax Press.

Upatissa Thera (~5th century) *Path of Freedom: Vimuttimagga*. Maharagama, Sri Lanka: The Saman Press, 1961.

The Samatha Trust, UK registered charity no. 1974, https://www.samatha.org

Wallace, B.A. (1999) The Buddhist tradition of Samatha: methods for refining and examining consciousness. *J. Consciousness Studies*, **6**(2-3), 175-87.

www.ingramcontent.com/pod-product-compliance
Ingram Content Group UK Ltd.
Pitfield, Milton Keynes, MK11 3LW, UK
UKHW060118010826
14089UKWH00004B/47

9 781838 099848